Bible Story Coloring Book

Directions for using this book

This big coloring book tells six stories from the Old ⌐ sections on the life of Jesus.

Use the tabs at the right to locate each story or sectio⌐ ⌐gh the book until you find the matching tab on the inside.

The pages are tear out so they can be reproduced for classroom use. Use them individually or in a montage by combining several separate pages to tell the whole story.

Old Testament Stories	Life of Jesus
Creation and Noah	Birth and Boyhood
Abraham and Isaac	Baptism and Sermon on the Mount
Jacob	Miracles
Joseph	Parables
Moses	Visit to Bethany and Last Supper
David	Arrest and Ascension

STANDARD PUBLISHING
Cincinnati, Ohio

Scriptures quoted from the *International Children's Bible, New Century Version*, copyright © 1986, 1988 by Word Publishing, Dallas, Texas 75039. Used by permission.

Standard Publishing, Cincinnati, Ohio.
A division of Standex International Corporation.
© 1994 Standard Publishing. All rights reserved.
Printed in the United States of America.

05 04 03 02   9 8 7
ISBN 0-7847-0171-7

Tabs (right margin):

- Creation and Noah
- Abraham and Isaac
- Jacob
- Joseph
- Moses
- David
- Birth and Boyhood
- Baptism and Sermon on the Mount
- Miracles
- Parables
- Visit to Bethany and Last Supper
- Arrest and Ascension

In the beginning God made the heavens and the earth. Grass and trees and flowers began to grow on the earth.

Genesis 1:1-12

God made the stars and moon to shine at night. He made the sun to shine in the daytime.

Genesis 1:14-18

God made fish to swim in the sea, and birds to fly in the air. He made all kinds of animals, some very small, and some very big.

Genesis 1:20-25

Last of all, God made a man, Adam, and a woman, Eve. God looked at all He had made and saw that it was very good.

Genesis 1:26-31

When God was creating He made a special garden which was called the Garden of Eden.

Genesis 2:8-10

Adam and Eve lived in the garden. Adam gave names to all the animals.

Genesis 2:19

God told Adam and Eve they could eat any fruit in the garden except for one kind. One day, the devil tempted Eve to eat that fruit.

Genesis 2:16, 17; 3:1-6

Adam also ate the fruit. Then Adam and Eve were ashamed, and tried
to hide from God. But no one can hide from God.

Genesis 3:6-8

Because they disobeyed Him, God sent Adam and Eve out of the
beautiful Garden of Eden.

Genesis 3:22-24

Many years passed. Many people now lived on the earth. They became very bad. God was sorry He had made people. *Genesis 6:5-7*

There was one good man, Noah. God told Noah to build a big ark-boat.
Noah and his sons obeyed God.

Genesis 6:8-22

When the ark-boat was made, God told Noah and his sons to bring two of every animal and put them into the ark-boat.

Genesis 7:7-9

Then God sent the rain. It rained forty days and forty nights. The whole earth was covered with water.

Genesis 7:10-24

Finally the water went down and the ark-boat rested on a mountain.
Noah, his family, and all the animals were glad to leave the ark.

Genesis 8:1-19

Noah and his family thanked God for caring for them. God promised
never to send a flood to cover the entire earth. God put a rainbow
in the sky as a sign of His promise.

Genesis 8:20-22; 9:11-13

"Sarah . . . gave birth to a son for Abraham in his old age. . . . Abraham named his son Isaac" (Genesis 21:2, 3).

Abram, a man of great faith, lived in a city called Ur. Abram was a rich man who had many sheep and cattle.

Genesis 11:27-30; 13:2

One day God spoke to Abram. He told Abram to leave Ur and go to a new land. Abram's family would become a great nation.   *Genesis 12:1-3*

Abram, his family, his servants, flocks, and herds all left Ur to go where God would lead them.

Genesis 11:31

They stopped at Haran, where Abram's father died. Then they went on
their way again until they finally came to Canaan.

Genesis 12:4, 5

Canaan was a beautiful land. Because of their many flocks and herds,
Abram and his nephew Lot divided the land.

Genesis 13:5-13

Again God promised He would make Abram's family a great nation. But Abram and his wife Sarai were getting old and had no children.

Genesis 13:14-18

God changed Abram's name to Abraham, which means father of many nations. His wife's name was changed to Sarah, mother of nations.

Genesis 17:1-8, 15, 16

Three strangers visited Abraham. He knew they were heavenly visitors.
After they had eaten a good meal, they told Sarah she would have a son.

Genesis 18:1-15

Just as God promised, Sarah had a son, and his parents named him Isaac.

Genesis 21:1-5

God said to Abraham, "Take Isaac, whom you love, and go to the land of Moriah. Build an altar and offer Isaac as a sacrifice."

Genesis 22:1, 2

braham obeyed God. When he was about to kill Isaac, God stopped him.
knew by this that Abraham had complete faith in Him.   *Genesis 22:3-19*

Abraham sent his servant to Haran to find Isaac a wife. At a well, the servant met Rebekah, a beautiful young woman.

Genesis 24:1-16

The servant took Rebekah back to Abraham's home. She and Isaac loved each other and had many happy years together as husband and wife.

Genesis 24:61-67

Isaac and Rebekah later became the parents of twin sons, Esau and Jacob.

Genesis 25:19-28

Isaac was a man of peace. When enemies took away his wells, he did not fight, but moved to another place where there was water. He knew the Lord would bless him wherever he went.

Genesis 26:17-25

"Jacob rose early in the morning. He took the stone he had slept on and set it up on its end. Then he poured olive oil on the top of it" (Genesis 28:18).

Isaac and Rebekah had twin sons, Esau and Jacob. Although they were twins, the boys were very different.

Genesis 25:20-26

Esau, the firstborn, liked to live outdoors and hunt. He was Isaac's favorite. Jacob preferred to stay at home and help his mother, Rebekah, and was her favorite.

Genesis 25:27, 28

One day, as Jacob was cooking soup, Esau came home very hungry. He asked for some of the soup. Jacob made a bargain with his brother.

Genesis 25:29, 30

"If you give me your birthright, I'll give you some soup," said
Jacob. Esau agreed, thinking only of his hunger, not of his rights
as the elder son.   *Genesis 25:31-34*

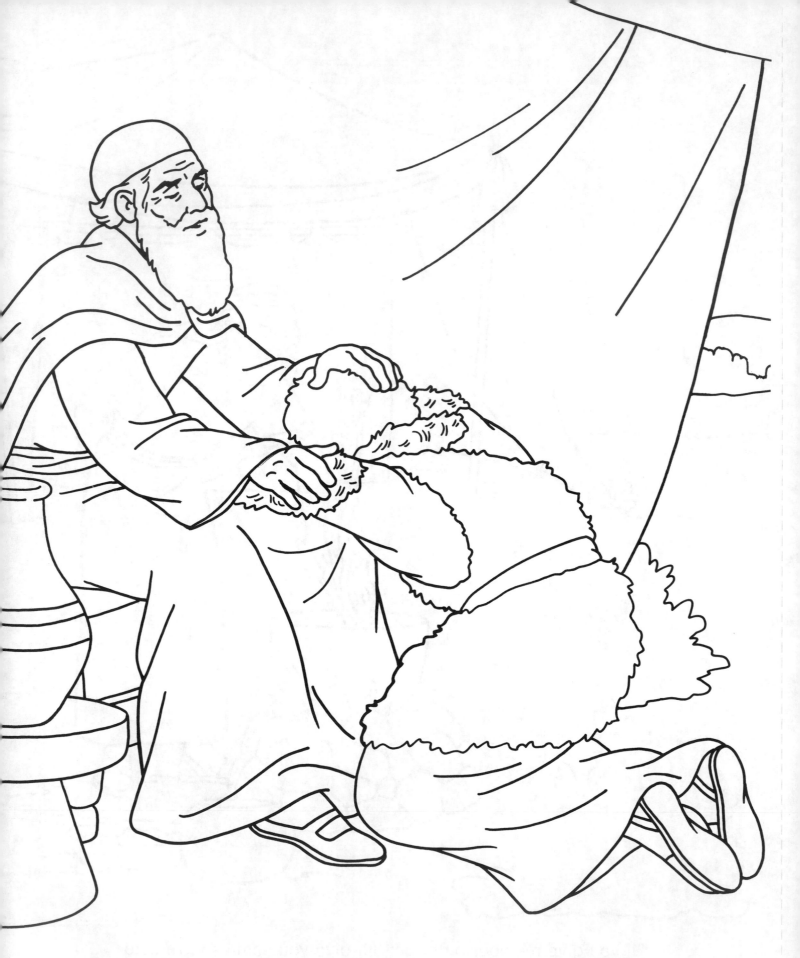

Isaac was old and blind. He called for Esau that he might give his firstborn son his blessing.

Genesis 27:1-5

With his mother's help, Jacob tricked Isaac into giving him Esau's blessing. Esau became angry and planned to kill Jacob.

Genesis 27:6-29, 41

Jacob traveled to Haran to seek a wife. One night he dreamed of angels on a ladder to Heaven. God spoke to Jacob and promised to bless him. Jacob called the place Bethel, meaning "house of God."

Genesis 28:1, 2, 10-19

Jacob stopped at a well in Haran. A beautiful young girl came to water her father's sheep. She was Rachel, daughter of Laban.

Genesis 29:1-14

Jacob agreed to work for Laban for seven years if he could marry Rachel.
But Laban tricked Jacob into marrying Leah, the older girl.

Genesis 29:15-26

In those days men often had more than one wife. Jacob worked seven more years in order to marry Rachel, whom he loved very much.

Genesis 29:27-30

After Jacob had worked for Laban twenty years, God told Jacob to go
back to his home.

Genesis 31:3

By now Jacob was a rich man with many children.

Genesis 31:17, 18

One night Jacob had a strange encounter. He wrestled with a heavenly visitor. The angel told Jacob he would now be called Israel, showing that he had power with God and with men.

Genesis 32:24-30

Jacob, fearing that Esau might still be angry, sent many presents to him. When Esau came out to greet him and his family, Jacob knew he had been forgiven.

Genesis 33:1-15

Finally, they reached the place where Isaac lived. How happy Isaac must have been to have Jacob and all his children home.

Genesis 35:27

"The king put Joseph in charge of all of Egypt"
(Genesis 41:43).

Joseph

Jacob gave his favorite son, Joseph, a coat of many colors.
Joseph's older brothers were jealous of him.   *Genesis 37:1-4*

Joseph had a dream that meant his family would someday bow down to him. This made his brothers more jealous than before.   *Genesis 37:5-11*

Joseph's older brothers were out in the fields looking after the sheep. Jacob sent Joseph to see how they were getting along.

Genesis 37:12-14

Joseph's brothers threw him in a pit. When some traders came by his brothers sold him to be a slave in Egypt. *Genesis 37:15-28*

The brothers went back to their father, Jacob, and told him a wild animal had killed Joseph. Jacob was very sad.　*Genesis 37:31-35*

Joseph was sold to a man named Potiphar. He put Joseph in charge of everything he owned. God blessed Joseph.

Genesis 39:1-6

Joseph was put in prison for something he did not do. Even here he was a good worker who trusted in God.

Genesis 39:20-23

When Pharaoh's chief butler and chief baker had strange dreams,
Joseph told them the meaning of their dreams.

Genesis 40

Later, Joseph was called to explain Pharaoh's dreams. There would be seven years of plenty and then seven years of famine. *Genesis 41:1-36*

Pharaoh put Joseph in charge of storing food for the years of famine.
In power, Joseph was second only to Pharaoh.   *Genesis 41:37-45*

Joseph's older brothers came to Egypt to buy food. They bowed down
to Joseph, not knowing who he was.   *Genesis 42:1-6*

The second time they came, Joseph gave his brothers a feast. He gave his younger brother, Benjamin, more than all the rest. *Genesis 43:26-34*

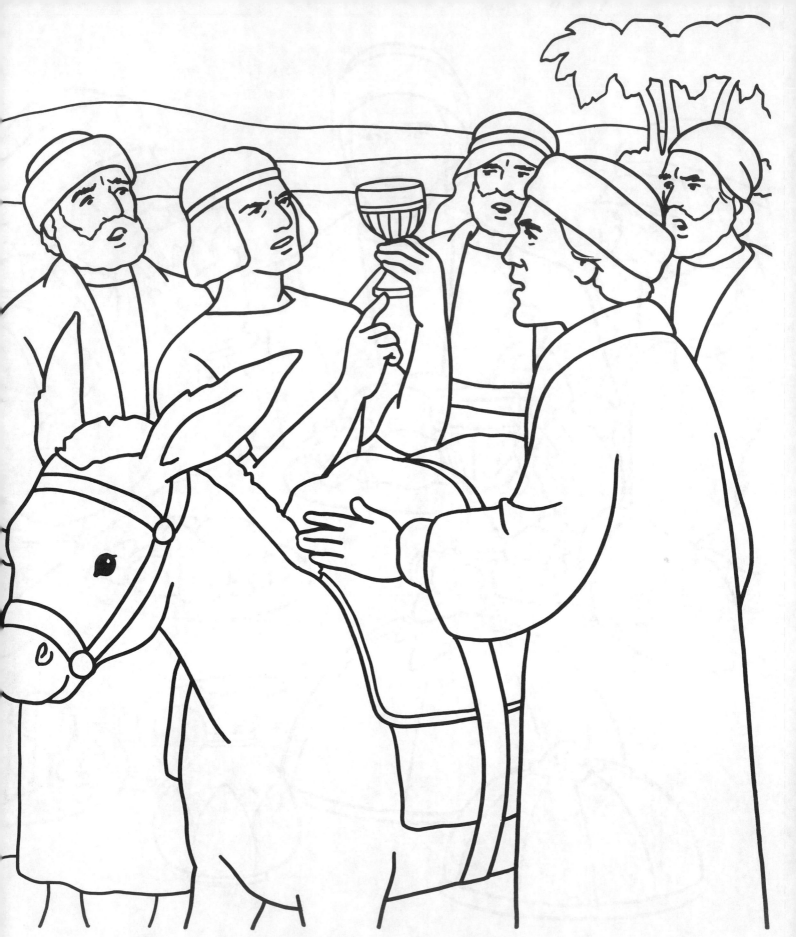

A servant put Joseph's silver cup in Benjamin's sack of grain.
Joseph sent the servant to make the brothers return.

Genesis 44:1-13

When Joseph saw his brothers were afraid, he told them who he was.
Joseph told his brothers that God had led him to Egypt. *Genesis 45:1-8*

Joseph's brothers brought their old father, Jacob, and all their families to live in the land of Egypt.

Genesis 46:26-34

"The king's daughter named him Moses, because she had pulled him out of the water" (Exodus 2:10).

Moses

God's people, the Israelites, were slaves in the land of Egypt.
Pharaoh ordered that all of their boy babies be killed.

Exodus 1:7-12, 22

One Israelite mother made a little basket bed for her baby boy. She took him to the river and hid him in the tall grass. *Exodus 2:1-4*

The princess of Egypt came to bathe in the river. She found the baby.
The baby's sister went to get her mother to take care of the baby.

Exodus 2:5-9

When the baby grew older he went to live in the palace with the princess. She named him Moses.

Exodus 2:10

When Moses was grown he went to Midian. At a well Moses chased away
some bad men and helped seven sisters water their sheep.   *Exodus 2:15-20*

Moses became a shepherd in Midian. One day, God spoke to him from a
burning bush. God told Moses to go back to Egypt to help his people.

Exodus 3:1-10

Moses told Pharaoh, "Let my people go!" But Pharaoh refused. Then God sent terrible plagues upon the people of Egypt. *Exodus 7:15–10:29*

The Israelites were told to kill a lamb and put the blood on the door. Then the death angel would pass over. The firstborn in each Egyptian family was killed. There was much sorrow in Egypt.

Exodus 12:3-13, 29, 30

That night, Pharaoh told the Israelites to leave Egypt. God led His people with a pillar of cloud by day and a pillar of fire by night.

Exodus 12:31; 13:17-22

When the Israelites came to the Red Sea they saw the Egyptians coming.
God caused the sea to divide and the Israelites escaped. *Exodus 14:19-31*

As the Israelites traveled through the wilderness they had no food.
God sent quail for meat and gave them manna for bread.

Exodus 16:11-15

Moses went to the top of Mt. Sinai to talk with God. God gave Moses
His Ten Commandments written on tables of stone. These were the laws
God wanted His people to obey.

Exodus 19:18-20; 20:1-17

While Moses talked with God, the people began to sin. They made a golden calf and bowed down to worship it.

Exodus 32:1-6

God told His people to build a tabernacle—a large, beautiful tent—
as a house of worship. This could be moved from place to place.

Exodus 40

After forty years of wandering, God's people were ready to enter the promised land. Moses climbed to the top of a large mountain to see this beautiful land, and died there on the mountaintop.   *Deuteronomy 34*

"Jesse answered, 'I still have the youngest son. He is out taking care of the sheep'" (1 Samuel 16:11).

David

David was a shepherd boy. Every day he led the sheep out to find
fresh water to drink and green grass to eat. *1 Samuel 16:11*

One day, as David kept the sheep, a lion came in and took a little lamb. David killed the lion and saved the lamb.   *1 Samuel 17:34, 35*

God told the prophet Samuel to go to Bethlehem to the home of Jesse. Here Samuel would find the next king of Israel.

1 Samuel 16:1

Jesse had eight sons. God chose the youngest one, David, to be the
next king. Samuel anointed David's head with oil.

1 Samuel 16:11-13

King Saul was sick. When he felt sick he liked to hear music. David was sent to play his harp for King Saul.

1 Samuel 16:14-23

Jesse's three oldest sons were soldiers in Saul's army. Jesse sent David to the camp with food for his brothers.   *1 Samuel 17:12-18*

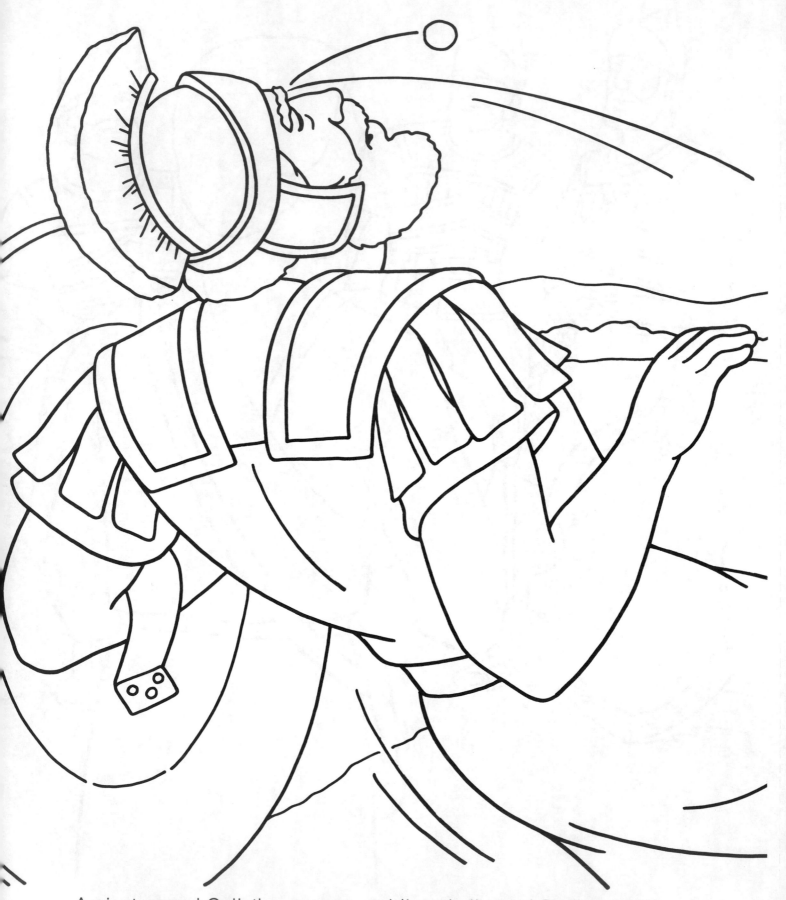

A giant named Goliath, an enemy soldier, challenged Saul's army to send a soldier out to fight him. The soldiers were afraid of Goliath.

1 Samuel 17:4-11

David was not afraid of Goliath. With God's help, David went out and killed Goliath with only a slingshot and stone.

1 Samuel 17:40-50

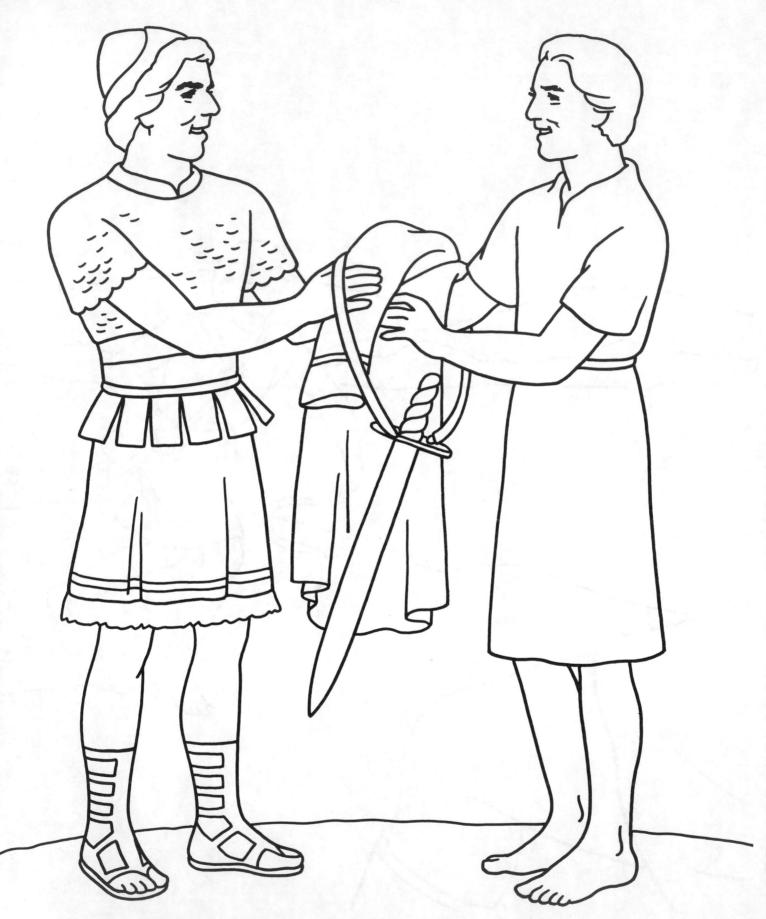

Jonathan, King Saul's son, became a good friend to David. Jonathan gave David some gifts. The young men promised to be friends always.

1 Samuel 18:1-4

King Saul was jealous because David was a hero. When David again played his harp, King Saul tried to kill him with a spear.

1 Samuel 18:5-11

David hid in a field. Jonathan shot some arrows in the field to warn
David to run from Saul. The two friends were sorry to part.

1 Samuel 20:35-42

Saul and his army were asleep. David and a friend went to Saul and took his water jar and spear but did not harm Saul. *1 Samuel 26:7-12*

David called to Saul from outside the camp. Because David spared his life, Saul agreed to stop trying to kill David.

1 Samuel 26:13-25

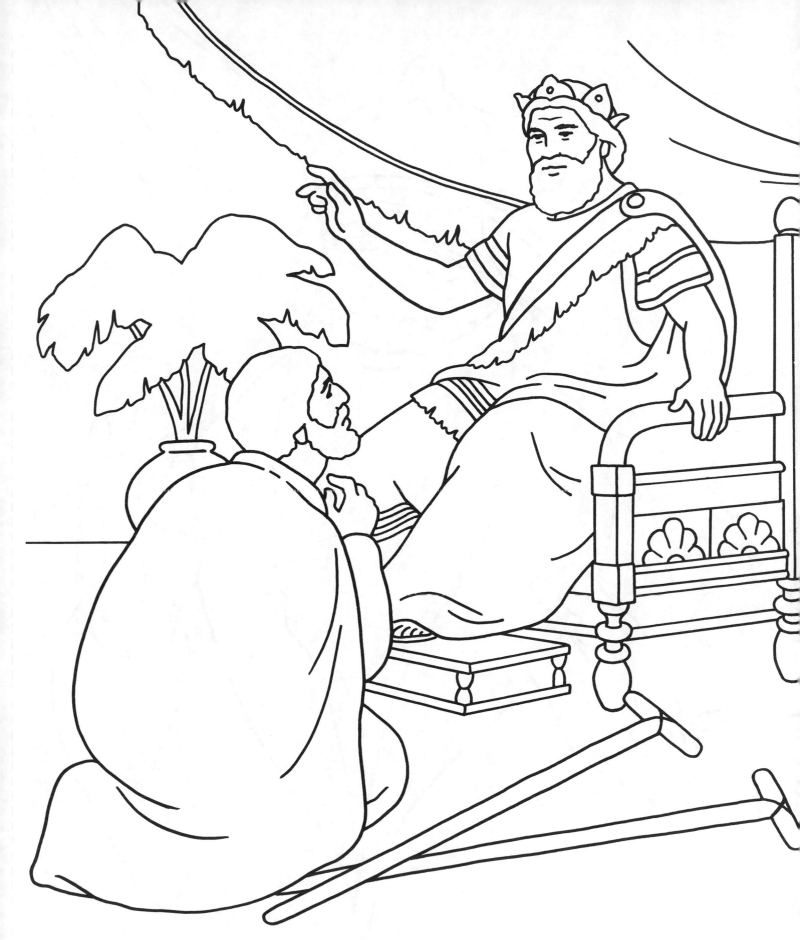

Many years passed. David was now king. He sent for Jonathan's son, who could not walk, to come to the palace to live as a prince.

2 Samuel 9

David was a good king over Israel. He served God and God blessed him and the nation. David was king for forty years.

2 Samuel 5:4

"You will name the son Jesus. Give him that name because he will save his people from their sins" (Matthew 1:21).

An angel of the Lord came to a young girl and said,
"Mary, you are going to be the mother of God's Son."

Luke 1:26-38

Mary married a man named Joseph.
They lived in the town of Nazareth.

Luke 2:4

Mary and Joseph went on a long trip to Bethlehem.
There they could find no room in the inn. *Luke 2:1-7*

Mary and Joseph had to stay in a stable.
Here Jesus, God's Son, was born.
Mary laid Him in a manger.   *Luke 2:6, 7*

While shepherds watched their sheep, an angel came to them.

"I bring you good news. God's Son is born," he said.

Luke 2:8-15

The shepherds came to the stable to see the baby Jesus.

They were happy to see God's Son, Jesus.

Luke 2:16-20

Later, Mary and Joseph took baby Jesus to the temple.
Old Simeon and Anna praised God that they could see His Son, Jesus.

Luke 2:22-38

Far away, some Wise-men saw a special star.
They followed it until they found the baby Jesus.

Matthew 2:1-9

The Wise-men came to Bethlehem with fine gifts for the baby Jesus.

Matthew 2:10-12

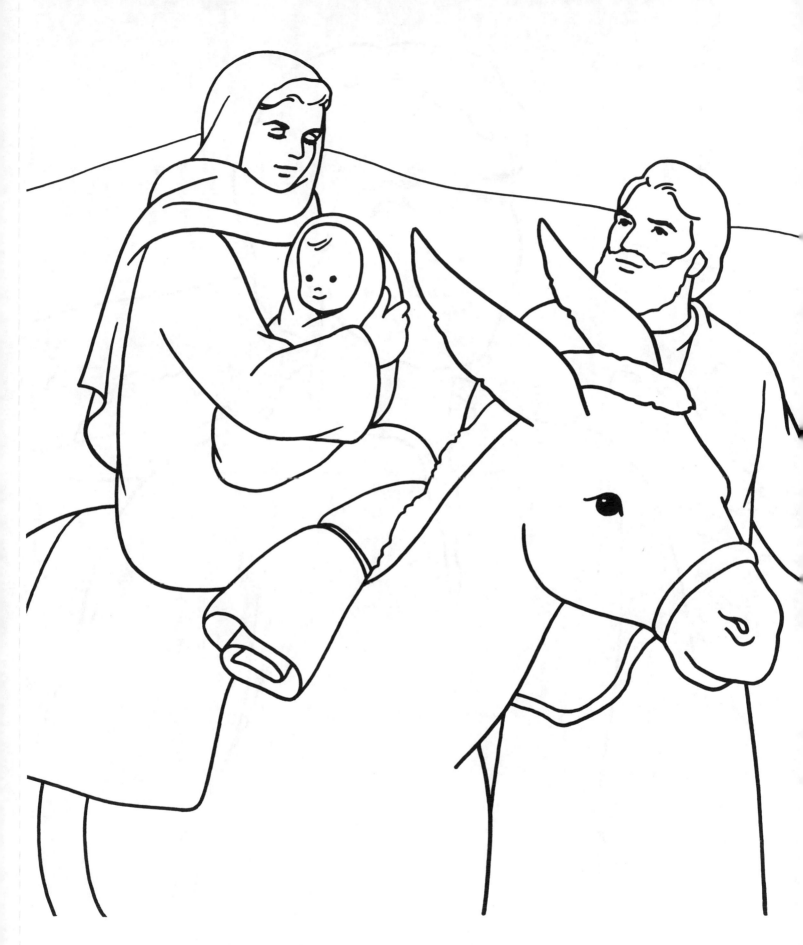

Joseph took Mary and her baby to Egypt to keep baby Jesus safe.

Matthew 2:13-15

When Jesus was twelve years old, He went with Mary and Joseph to Jerusalem to worship God. *Luke 2:41, 42*

When they missed Jesus, Mary and Joseph found Him in the temple.
He was asking and answering questions.

Luke 2:43-50

Jesus grew in wisdom, in stature, in favor with God,
and in favor with man.   *Luke 2:52.*

"Jesus . . . went up on a hill and sat down. His followers came to him. Jesus taught the people" (Matthew 5:1, 2).

Baptism and Sermon on the Mount

When Jesus was about thirty years old, He came
to the Jordan River to be baptized.

God said, "This is my beloved Son.
I am well pleased with Him."

Mark 1:4-11

The devil tried to get Jesus to do some wrong things.

Jesus would do no wrong for He is the Son of God.

Luke 4:1-13

Andrew brought his brother, Simon Peter, to meet Jesus.

John 1:35-42

Jesus told Philip and Nathaniel that they would see Him do great things.

John 1:43-51

Nicodemus, a leader of the Jews, came to see Jesus at night.

John 3:1-17

Jesus talked to a woman of Samaria about the living water.

John 4:5-30, 39-42

Jesus called Peter, Andrew, James, and John to become
fishers of men.

They left their fishing nets and followed Jesus.

Mark 1:16-21

Matthew was a tax collector.

When Jesus said, "Follow me," Matthew left his work and followed Jesus.

Matthew 9:9

Jesus had much to do while He was here on earth.

He chose twelve men to be His special helpers.
They were called apostles. *Luke 6:12-16*

One day, Jesus spoke to a great crowd of people on a mountainside.
He told them many things about the kingdom of Heaven.

Matthew 5, 6, 7

"Jesus went to a town called Nain. . . . A mother, who was a widow, had lost her only son. . . . Jesus said, 'Young man, I tell you, get up!' And the son sat up and began to talk. Then Jesus gave him back to his mother" (Luke 7:11-15).

Jesus and His friends were invited to a large wedding feast.
After a time, the wine was all gone.

Jesus told the servants to fill six jars with water.
When the water was poured out, it became wine.
This was Jesus' first miracle. *John 2:1-12*

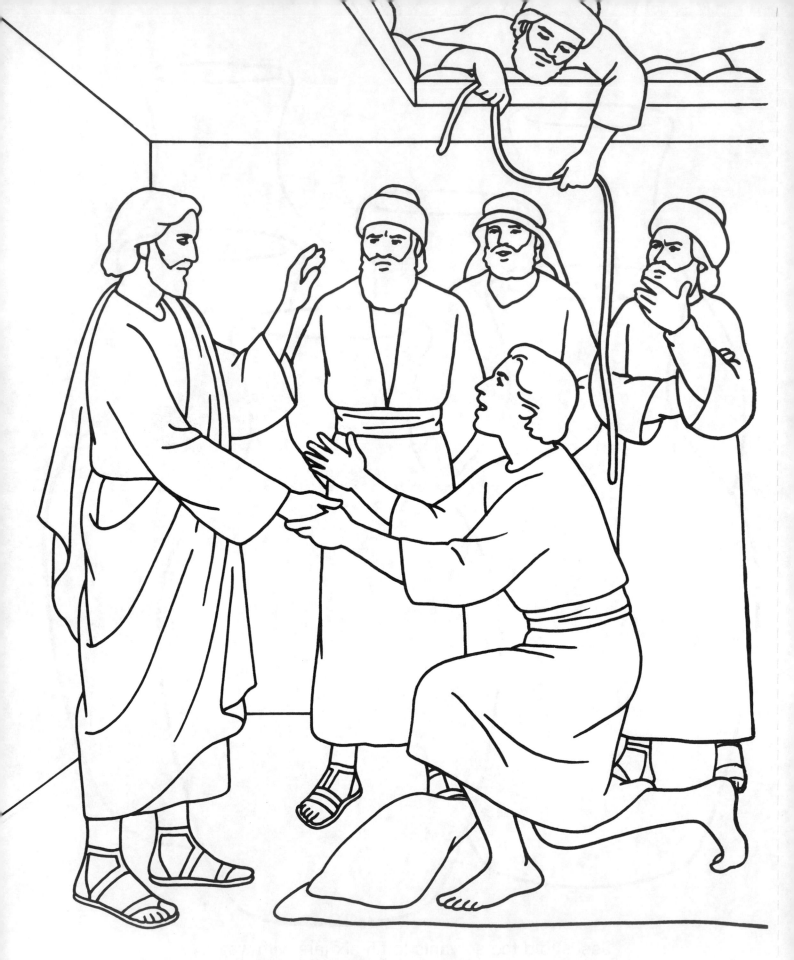

Four men brought their sick friend to Jesus.
The house was so full that they could not get near Jesus.

The men made a hole in the roof and let their sick friend down.
Jesus made him get well right away.

Mark 2:1-12

At the pool of Bethesda, Jesus told a sick man to pick
up his bed and walk.
The man did as Jesus said. He was well!   *John 5:1-9*

A young man who had died was going to be buried.
Jesus said to the body, "Young man, wake up!"
The man got up. He was alive!   *Luke 7:11-17*

Jesus and His helpers were on the Sea of Galilee when a storm came up.
Jesus told the wind and waves to be still. They obeyed Him. *Mark 4:35-41*

A little girl had died.
Jesus took her hand and said, "Little girl, arise."
The girl opened her eyes, got up, and walked.

Luke 8:41, 42, 49-56

A large crowd that followed Jesus had had nothing to eat all day.
A small boy gave his lunch to Jesus.

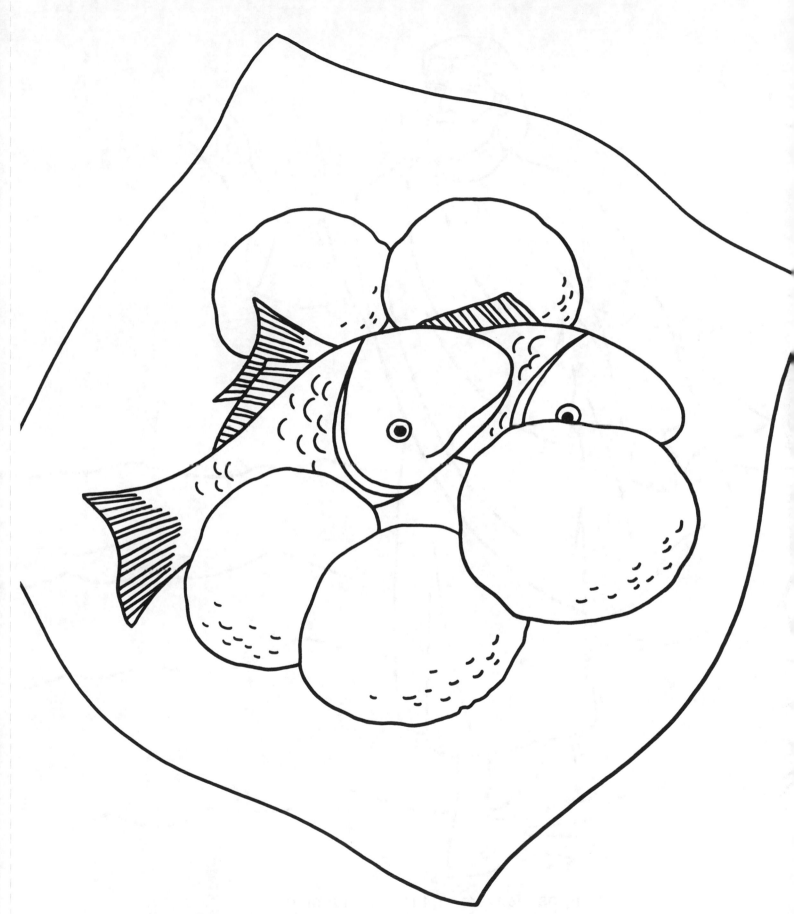

Jesus took the five loaves and two fish and asked God to bless it.
Then He made enough food to feed everyone, with some left over.

John 6:1-14

The apostles were on the sea in a storm.
Suddenly they saw Jesus.
He was walking on the water!

Mark 6:45-52

Peter, James, and John went with Jesus to a mountaintop.
Jesus' face and clothing began to shine.
Then Moses and Elijah came to talk with Jesus. *Mark 9:2-8*

Jesus put clay on the eyes of a man born blind.
The man washed off the clay as Jesus told him.
He could see!

John 9:1-38

Jesus made ten sick men well again.
Only one man came back to say thank You to Jesus.

Luke 17:11-19

As Jesus passed by, a blind beggar called, "Jesus, help me!"
Jesus told the man his faith had made him well.
The man could see!

Mark 10:46-52

"Jesus . . . always used stories to teach people" (Matthew 13:34).

Parables

Jesus told the story of a farmer who planted some seeds.
Only the seeds that fell on the good soil grew into plants.

Matthew 13:3-8, 18-23

The enemies of a certain farmer planted some weeds among his wheat. When the farmer harvested his wheat, he burned the weeds.

Matthew 13:24-30, 36-43

When a man could not pay back a large amount of money he owed,
the king forgave him and did not punish him.

The same man would not forgive another man when he owed a very
    small amount of money.
When the king heard this, he had the first man put in jail.

Matthew 18:23-35

A certain man was beat up and robbed by some bad men.
They left the poor, hurt man beside the road.

Two men passed by but would not stop to help the man.
Then a man from the country of Samaria stopped to take care
of the hurt man.

The Samaritan man took the hurt man to an inn.
He paid the innkeeper to take care of the man until he was well.
The Samaritan was a good neighbor.

Luke 12:25-37

A shepherd had one hundred sheep.
One night, one little sheep got lost.
The shepherd went out to find the lost sheep.

When the shepherd found his sheep, he carried it home.
He called in his friends to tell them how happy he was to find the
lost sheep.

Luke 15:4-6

A father had two sons.
The younger son took his share of the father's money and went away.
When the money was gone, the son had nothing to eat.

The younger son was sorry he had left home.
He went back to his father and said, "I'm sorry."
The father was happy that his son came back because he loved
   his son very much.

Luke 15:11-24

When a rich man went away, he gave his servants some money to use.
Two of his servants used their money to earn more money.
The third did not even try to earn more money. He was a lazy servant.

Matthew 25:14-30

A rich farmer had so much grain that he had to build bigger barns.
God was not pleased with the man because he trusted in his own riches.

Luke 12:16-21

A wise man built his house on a rock.
When the storms came, the house did not fall.
People who do what Jesus says to do are like the wise man.

A foolish man built his house on the sand.
When the storms came, the house fell down.
People who do not do what Jesus says to do are like
    the foolish man.

Matthew 7:24-27

"Mary brought in a pint of very expensive perfume made from pure nard. She poured the perfume on Jesus' feet, and then she wiped his feet with her hair" (John 12:3).

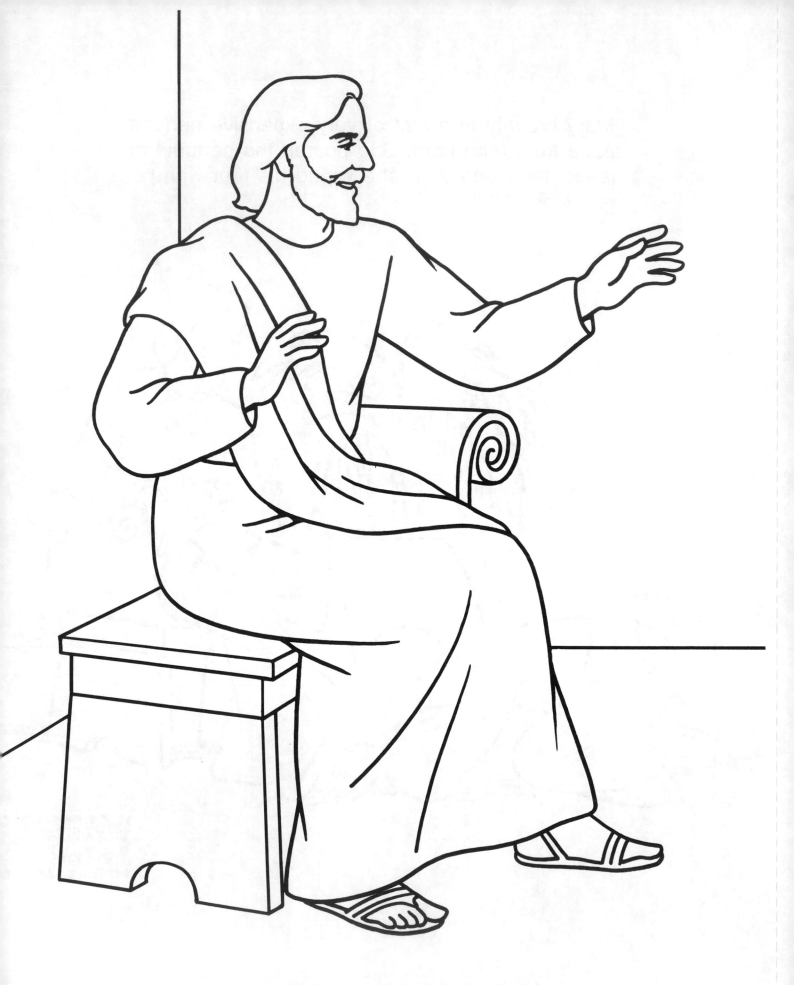

Jesus liked to visit in the home of Mary and Martha.

Martha cooked the dinner while Mary sat and listened to Jesus.

Luke 10:38-42

Some boys and girls wanted to see Jesus.
His helpers thought He was too busy.

Jesus loved the children.
"Let the children come to me," He said.
"Do not stop them."   *Mark 10:13-16*

A rich young man came running to Jesus.
The man wanted to know how to get eternal life.

The young man went away sad.
He was not willing to give up his riches to follow Jesus.
He loved his money too much.

Matthew 19:16-30

A tax collector named Zacchaeus wanted to see Jesus.
Zacchaeus climbed up into a tree because he was too short
to see over the crowd.

Jesus saw Zacchaeus and called him to come down.
Zacchaeus became a friend of Jesus.   *Luke 19:1-10*

Jesus again ate in the home of Mary, Martha,
and their brother, Lazarus.

To show her love for Jesus, Mary put some sweet-smelling
perfume on Jesus' feet.

John 12:1-8

Jesus rode into Jerusalem on a colt.
Many people put palm branches or their own cloaks on the road.

"Blessed is the King that comes in the name of the Lord!"
shouted the happy people.

Luke 19:35-44

Jesus said that the poor woman who gave only two small coins loved
God most of all, because she gave all that she had.   *Luke 21:1-4*

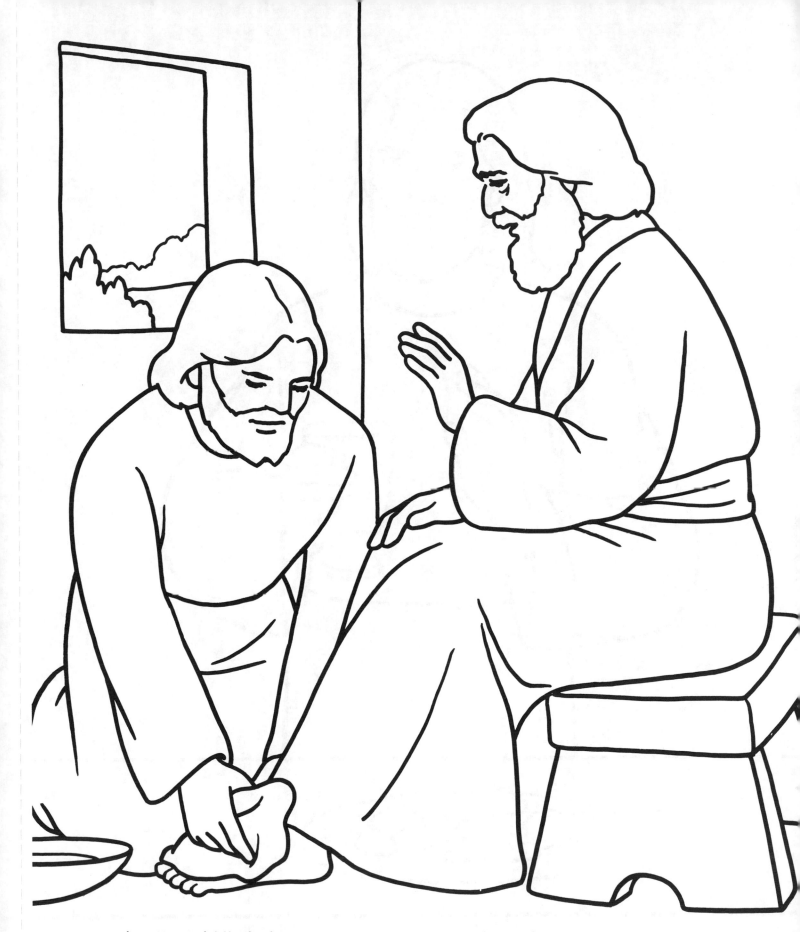

Jesus and His helpers met to eat a special meal.
Jesus took the place of a servant and washed the feet of His helpers.

John 13:1-17

After the special meal, Jesus gave His helpers bread and grape juice.
When they ate this they were to be reminded of His death.
Christians take this "Lord's Supper" today. *Luke 22:17-20; 1 Corinthians 11:23-26*

"The man said, 'Don't be afraid. You are looking for Jesus . . . He has risen from death. He is not here. Look, here is the place they laid him'" (Mark 16:6).

Jesus and His apostles went to the Garden of Gethsemane.
Jesus wanted to pray to His Father in Heaven.

As Jesus prayed, His helpers fell asleep.

Matthew 26:36-46

Judas, one of the apostles, brought some men who were
enemies of Jesus.

The enemies of Jesus grabbed Him.
They led him away to be tried by the rulers.

Matthew 26:47-56

Even though Jesus did nothing wrong, Pilate ordered Him
to be killed on a cross.

John 18:28–19:16

The soldiers made a man named Simon carry the cross for Jesus.

Luke 23:26

On a hill called Calvary, Jesus was put to death.
Jesus' friends were very sad.

The sky became black! The earth shook! Rocks were torn apart!
Everyone was afraid! A Roman soldier said, "This was the Son of God."

Luke 23:33-49

On the third day after Jesus died, some women came
to the place where He was buried.

An angel said, "He is not here. He is alive!"
The women hurried to tell the good news.

Luke 24:1-10

A woman named Mary did not know Jesus until He spoke her name.

John 20:1, 11-18

That same day, Jesus walked and talked with two men.
How excited they were when they knew it was Jesus!

Luke 24:13-35

Jesus' helpers were in a certain room.
Suddenly, Jesus was in the room with them!

Jesus asked for something to eat.
The helpers knew He was really alive again!

Luke 24:36-48

After forty days, Jesus was ready to go back to Heaven.
As His helpers watched Him go up, an angel said,
"Some day, Jesus will come back again."

Luke 24:50-52; Acts 1:2-11